Spotlight on
Kids Can Code

Why Are There So Many

PROGRAMMING LANGUAGES?

Patricia Harris

PowerKiDS press

New York

Published in 2018 by The Rosen Publishing Group, Inc.
29 East 21st Street, New York, NY 10010

Copyright © 2018 by The Rosen Publishing Group, Inc.

All rights reserved. No part of this book may be reproduced in any form without permission in writing from the publisher, except by a reviewer.

First Edition

Editor: Elizabeth Krajnik
Book Design: Michael J. Flynn

Photo Credits: Cover TongRo Images Inc/TongRo Images/Getty Images; p. 5 Ozgur Coskun/Shutterstock.com; p. 7 https://commons.wikimedia.org/wiki/File:Two_women_operating_ENIAC.gif; p. 9 Matthew Naythons/ The LIFE Images Collection/Getty Images; p. 10 Daisy Daisy/Shutterstock.com; p. 12 https://commons. wikimedia.org/wiki/File:The_Cubetto_Playset.jpg; p. 13 courtesy of the LOGO Foundation; p. 15 monstArr/ Shutterstock.com; p. 17 Rawpixel.com/Shutterstock.com; p. 18 wavebreakmedia/Shutterstock.com; p. 19 http://www.economist.com/; p. 21 (Scratch screenshot) Scratch is developed by the Lifelong Kindergarten Group at the MIT Media Lab. See http://scratch.mit.edu.

Library of Congress Cataloging-in-Publication Data

Names: Harris, Patricia, 1943 October 17- author.
Title: Why are there so many programming languages? / Patricia Harris.
Description: New York : PowerKids Press, [2018] | Series: Spotlight on kids
  can code | Includes index.
Identifiers: LCCN 2016056863| ISBN 9781508155201 (pbk. book) | ISBN
  9781508154259 (6 pack) | ISBN 9781508155089 (library bound book)
Subjects: LCSH: Programming languages (Electronic computers)–Juvenile
  literature. | Computer programming–Juvenile literature. | CYAC:
  Programming languages (Computers)
Classification: LCC QA76.7 .H3775 2018 | DDC 005.26/2–dc23
LC record available at https://lccn.loc.gov/2016056863

Manufactured in the United States of America

CPSIA Compliance Information: Batch #BS17PK: For Further Information contact Rosen Publishing, New York, New York at 1-800-237-9932

Contents

The Right Language for the Job 4

The First Programmable Computer 6

Early Programming Languages..........8

BASIC.................................10

Educational Programming Languages....12

Object-Oriented Programming.........14

Relational Databases and SQL........16

Scripting Languages.................18

Block Coding........................20

The Future of Programming...........22

Glossary 23

Index...............................24

Websites............................24

The Right Language for the Job

Let's say you need a small load of soil for your garden. What type of truck would you need to carry the soil? You wouldn't use a huge dump truck that holds 10 tons of dirt, but a small sports car wouldn't be big enough. You'd need a pickup truck. Any style or brand of pickup would work as long as it has the basic features needed for the job.

If all computers reduce data to the 1s and 0s of the **binary number system**, then why are there so many programming languages? Different languages fill certain needs and solve certain problems. As computer **hardware** became more advanced and the types of users changed, coders created new languages. Coders and computer users need to choose the right type of language for each job.

Using the right type of programming language is like using the right type of tool to complete a physical task. For example, you wouldn't use a spoon to add dirt to a garden. You'd use a shovel.

The First Programmable Computer

Before the 1950s, during a time when computers were still new devices, a few computer systems could complete a series of operations. One of these computer systems was the ENIAC. John Presper Eckert Jr. and John Mauchly designed the ENIAC to help the military during World War II and it was introduced to the public on February 15, 1946. While it could do some fundamental computer functions, it could not store programs. People had to manually change switches and cables to program the ENIAC.

The ENIAC's first programmers were women: Kathleen McNulty Mauchly Antonelli, Jean Jennings Bartik, Frances Snyder Holberton, Marlyn Wescoff Meltzer, Frances Bilas Spence, and Ruth Lichterman Teitelbaum. They made the changes necessary to enter a program and **debugged** programs by finding problems inside the machine.

When new computer systems were developed in the 1950s and 1960s, the need for new high-level languages developed.

Jean Jennings Bartik (left) and Frances Bilas Spence (right) are pictured here setting up a part of the ENIAC at the Moore School of Electrical Engineering at the University of Pennsylvania.

Breaking the Code

When the ENIAC was first introduced, it was used for a secret military project. But when it was released to the public in 1946, the names of its programmers were never made known. For almost 70 years these women went unnoticed. In 2013, Kathy Kleiman, John Palfreman, and Kate McMahon made a 20-minute documentary titled *The Computers* about these pioneers in the field of computer programming.

Early Programming Languages

During the 1950s and 1960s, computer scientists developed three languages that later served as the basis for many other programming languages—LISP, FORTRAN, and BASIC. LISP and FORTRAN are the oldest high-level programming languages that are still used today.

LISP was developed in 1958 for work in artificial intelligence. Artificial intelligence is an area of computer science in which computers act like the human mind by using **statistics** and **logic** to solve problems. LISP uses lists that are linked together to form programs. The language also introduced programming ideas such as trees, which are a type of **data structure**, and **conditionals**.

John W. Backus developed FORTRAN, which stands for FORmula TRANslation, in 1957 for use in math, engineering, and science. He first invented it to reduce the amount of code needed to do a task. Backus wrote FORTRAN to be used on many different types of computers.

John McCarthy was the inventor of LISP, which is short for LISt Processor.

BASIC

BASIC, which stands for Beginner's All-purpose Symbolic Instruction Code, is the language that Microsoft was built on. It was the first language that could be used on a **time-share computer** to give the coder instant output, or information produced by a computer. It was a good language for beginners because its limited keywords, or words that cause something to happen in the program, are all English words. One of those keywords, "GOTO," causes the program to jump to a certain line in the code.

The use of computers in education was a whole new area of programming and it required new languages. In the 1960s, people developed three programming languages to support education: TUTOR, PILOT, and Logo. While TUTOR and PILOT are not related to the three major languages of this period, Logo was developed from LISP.

This GOTO statement in Atari BASIC tells the computer to print a page saying "Hello World" over and over until the programmer writes a code telling it to stop.

Educational Programming Languages

Computer scientists developed TUTOR for use in computer-assisted instruction. The language has commands that judge whether an answer is right and a graphics display on its companion **terminal**, which is known as the PLATO system. Later, people also used TUTOR to create games.

PILOT is another language developed for computer-assisted instruction. Its main purpose was to allow the instructor to give tests on different types of computers. In a way, PILOT was developed to replace textbooks because teachers could use the language to write interactive programs to instruct their students.

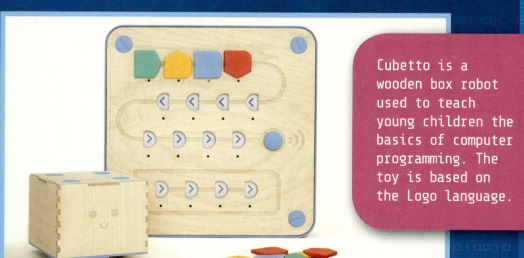

Cubetto is a wooden box robot used to teach young children the basics of computer programming. The toy is based on the Logo language.

Logo is a language developed to teach principles related to LISP. Logo is best known for its turtle graphics. Students can use the language to write code to make an on-screen turtle move and draw geometric designs. Teachers used the language in schools to teach children programming and math.

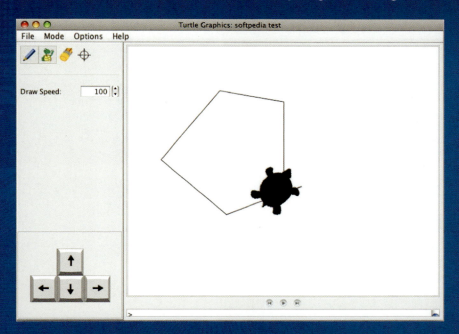

Breaking the Code

To program Cubetto, children place coding blocks into positions on a control board. Each block means something different: green for forward, yellow for left, red for right, and blue to create longer code lines. Once the blocks have been placed on the board, children press a button and Cubetto follows the program's instructions. The goal of Cubetto is to teach children how to code without screens.

Object-Oriented Programming

New **technology** and new uses for it call for new ways of thinking about programming. A great change in programming happened in the 1970s and 1980s and still affects us today. This era saw the beginning of object-oriented programming with the programming language C, which packages data into objects that can be manipulated.

Computer scientists later developed C++ and other forms of the language, but all versions of C are object-oriented. That means coders focus on the objects they want to work with rather than the logic they need to use to complete a task. C languages are powerful, but they can be hard to use. If you want to write the code for a video game that has a lot of graphics, C is the best language to use.

Pascal is another object-oriented language from this time period. Pascal is not as powerful as C, but it is easier to use.

The family of C languages allows for complex programming, but the code doesn't look much like English.

```
                    continue;
                }
                float du = (tiles[i] % 16) * s;
                float dv = (tiles[i] / 16) * s;
                int flip = ao[i][0] + ao[i][3] > ao[i][1] + ao[i][2];
                for (int v = 0; v < 6; v++) {
                    int j = flip ? flipped[i][v] : indices[i][v];
                    *(d++) = x + n * positions[i][j][0];
                    *(d++) = y + n * positions[i][j][1];
                    *(d++) = z + n * positions[i][j][2];
                    *(d++) = normals[i][0];
                    *(d++) = normals[i][1];
                    *(d++) = normals[i][2];
                    *(d++) = du + (uvs[i][j][0] ? b : a);
                    *(d++) = dv + (uvs[i][j][1] ? b : a);
                    *(d++) = ao[i][j];
                    *(d++) = light[i][j];
                }
            }
        }
    }

    void make_cube(
        float *data, float ao[6][4], float light[6][4],
        int left, int right, int top, int bottom, int front, int back,
        float x, float y, float z, float n, int w)
    {
        int wleft = blocks[w][0];
        int wright = blocks[w][1];
        int wtop = blocks[w][2];
        int wbottom = blocks[w][3];
        int wfront = blocks[w][4];
        int wback = blocks[w][5];
        make_cube_faces(
            data, ao, light,
            left, right, top, bottom, front, back,
            wleft, wright, wtop, wbottom, wfront, wback,
            x, y, z, n);
    }

    void make_plant(
        float *data, float ao, float light,
        float px, float py, float pz, float n, int w, float rotation) {

        static const float positions[4][4][3] = {
            {{ 0, -1, -1}, { 0, -1, +1}, { 0, +1, -1}, { 0, +1, +1}},
            {{ 0, -1, -1}, { 0, -1, +1}, { 0, +1, -1}, { 0, +1, +1}},
            {{-1, -1,  0}, {-1, +1,  0}, {+1, -1,  0}, {+1, +1,  0}},
            {{-1, -1,  0}, {-1, +1,  0}, {+1, -1,  0}, {+1, +1,  0}}
        };
        static const float normals[4][3] = {
            {-1, 0, 0},
            {+1, 0, 0},
            {0, 0, -1},
```

Relational Databases and SQL

As **databases** became more advanced, they required new programming languages. Relational databases, which recognize the relationships between data, required a new language called structured query language (SQL). With this new language, programmers didn't have to make new software programs for companies who used these databases.

The most used command in SQL is "SELECT," which gathers data from a table or tables. The coder has to tell the "SELECT" command where to look for the data they want to choose. The language has ways to enter data, add to it, and make changes. It also uses Boolean logic—which allows the programmer to find relationships between data using special commands—to compare pieces of data. Almost all database systems use SQL today, but some use special versions. The underlying language is still SQL.

Databases that use SQL are used in many organizations today. The healthcare industry often uses these databases because of the high volume of data.

Scripting Languages

Scripting languages are programming languages that interpret and execute the programmer's commands one at a time. Scripting languages have special programs called scripts that do some of the work for a programmer. These types of programming languages have been around since the earliest computers.

Since the 1990s, several new scripting languages have been developed to keep up with changes in technology and the ways people use computers. HTML, PHP, Java, JavaScript, and Python are some of these languages. Older

languages were improved to keep up with advances in technology. Scripting is used today for developing web pages and, in some cases, games.

HTML is the standard for creating websites. When you go to a website through your browser, you see either http:// or https:// before the rest of the website address. This tells you that a server is sending an HTML file to your computer or mobile device.

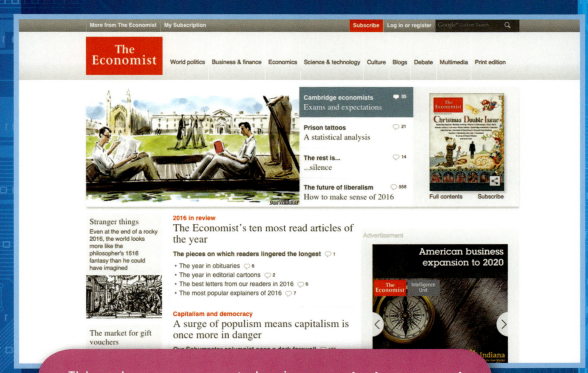

This web page was created using a **content management system** called Drupal. The people changing the information on the web page only have to enter the text and pictures. Drupal does the rest!

Block Coding

Block coding is code that has been grouped together in some way. A person can write code by dragging blocks—which are often shaped like puzzle pieces—to a code area, rather than writing text-based code. This can help learners understand coding without struggling with a more advanced language.

Block coding is a part of most programming languages. Blocks may be set off by a special character or indenting, but they are groups of text. Graphical or visual programming languages put blocks in puzzle pieces that can be connected, but the coder still has to understand the principles of programming.

People have criticized block coding because most advanced programming is done using text. Some advanced coders think beginners should have to use coding **syntax** and learn from the mistakes they make when typing.

Scratch is a visual programming language designed to create animations and simple games. This code creates a flying bat.

Breaking the Code

In recent years, block coding has become even more popular as a way to teach young children how to code without teaching them text-based programming concepts. Teaching children how to program with text-based programming languages can be difficult. Today, there are several online games, like CodeMonkey, that help children progress from block to text-based coding.

The Future of Programming

Why are there so many programming languages? People have developed different languages to meet needs, to solve problems, to work with new types of computers, and to make programming understandable to new users.

Only a few people were involved in programming when computers were new and computer tasks were limited. However, as computer hardware became more advanced and the problems people wanted to solve changed, people wrote new programming languages. Today, many people have computers and mobile devices and use the results of decades of computer programmers' hard work and ingenuity. Many people also want to create personal web pages, simple games, and apps for smart devices.

Today, many elementary school students are taught computer programming in the classroom. These kids may discover an even easier way to make computer programming more understandable.

Glossary

binary number system: A system that represents numbers using two digits (0 and 1).

conditional: A statement that is either true or false depending on the situation.

content management system: An interface that allows users to publish content directly to the web.

database: A collection of data that is organized and used on a computer.

data structure: Any of the methods of organizing pieces of data in a computer.

debug: To find and remove the mistakes from a computer program.

hardware: The physical parts of a computer system.

logic: The science that studies the formal processes used in thinking and reasoning.

statistics: The branch of mathematics dealing with the collection, analysis, and presentation of numerical data.

syntax: How words are arranged to form a sentence.

technology: The way that people do something using tools and the tools that they use.

terminal: A computer or display connected to a computer system that is used for receiving and viewing information.

time-share computer: A computer that can be used by many people at different locations at the same time.

Index

A
Antonelli, Kathleen McNulty Mauchly, 6
artificial intelligence, 8

B
Backus, John W., 8
Bartik, Jean Jennings, 6, 7
BASIC, 8, 10, 11
binary number system, 4
block coding, 20, 21
Boolean logic, 16

C
C, 14
C++, 14
CodeMonkey, 21
Computers, The, 7
Cubetto, 12, 13

D
databases, 16, 17
Drupal, 19

E
Eckert, John Presper Jr., 6
ENIAC, 6, 7

F
FORTRAN, 8

H
Holberton, Frances Snyder, 6
HTML, 18, 19

J
Java, 18
JavaScript, 18

L
LISP, 8, 9, 11, 13
Logo, 11, 12, 13

M
Mauchly, John, 6
McCarthy, John, 9
Meltzer, Marlyn Wescoff, 6

Microsoft, 10
Moore School of Electrical Engineering, 7

P
Pascal, 14
PHP, 18
PILOT, 11, 12
PLATO system, 12
Python, 18

S
Scratch, 21
scripting languages, 18, 19
Spence, Frances Bilas, 6, 7
SQL, 16, 17

T
Teitelbaum, Ruth Lichterman, 6
TUTOR, 11, 12

W
World War II, 6

Websites

Due to the changing nature of Internet links, PowerKids Press has developed an online list of websites related to the subject of this book. This site is updated regularly. Please use this link to access the list: www.powerkidslinks.com/skcc/lang